His Story!

Getting to Know the Man
on the Cross Through
First-Person Interviews

By Robert Esco, Jr.

TEACH Services, Inc.
P U B L I S H I N G
www.TEACHServices.com • (800) 367-1844

World rights reserved. This book or any portion thereof may not be copied or reproduced in any form or manner whatever, except as provided by law, without the written permission of the publisher, except by a reviewer who may quote brief passages in a review.

The author assumes full responsibility for the accuracy of all facts and quotations as cited in this book. The opinions expressed in this book are the author's personal views and interpretations, and do not necessarily reflect those of the publisher.

This book is provided with the understanding that the publisher is not engaged in giving spiritual, legal, medical, or other professional advice. If authoritative advice is needed, the reader should seek the counsel of a competent professional.

Copyright © 2021 Robert Esco, Jr.

Copyright © 2021 TEACH Services, Inc.

ISBN-13: 978-1-4796-0652-8 (Paperback)

ISBN-13: 978-1-4796-0653-5 (ePub)

Library of Congress Control Number: 2016910002

Unless otherwise indicated, all Scripture quotations are from the King James Version (KJV).

Scripture quotations marked NKJV are from the New King James Version®. Copyright © 1982 by Thomas Nelson. Used by permission. All rights reserved.

No part of this publication may be reproduced, stored in a retrieval system or transmitted in any form or by any means—electronic, mechanical, photocopying, recording, or otherwise—without prior written permission.

www.TEACHServices.com • (800) 367-1844

Contents

1. At the Cross — 7
2. Spectators in the Crowd — 24
3. A Shift in the Weather — 44
4. "It Is Finished" — 53
5. At Rest — 61
6. The Night Vigil — 68
7. The Dawn's Early Light — 76
8. In the Upper Room — 83
9. A Personal Interview — 95
10. The Story Goes On — 105

Introduction

The writers of the Gospels tell the story of Jesus, focusing on the week of Jesus' crucifixion. It is a story that has the potential of touching every human being. Yet, it is more than a story—it is actual events; it is history that is "His story." However, first century writers did not include the kind of detail that modern readers expect. The biblical story comes across as if written in black and white. This little book attempts to add color, telling His story from the point of view of one interviewing people who knew the crucified one. Reflected in their purported expressions are the love, bravery, kindness, forgiveness and strength of Jesus. Even in using the imagination to capture their thoughts and feelings, the author has done his best to present an accurate and truthful account of the events with the hope that it will inspire readers and not merely entertain them. He respectfully asks that readers allow him a little latitude in filling in some of the spaces. What follows is then Jesus' story, focusing on His crucifixion and resurrection, as recounted through the voice of first-century eyewitnesses.

1

At the Cross

"Who is this man?" I asked aloud as I watched a fatigued and beaten figure stretched out upon two connected pieces of rough-hewn timber forming a cross and then fixed in place by spikes through His hands and feet. It was the horrible finale to a long, humiliating parade through the city streets—a man carrying the object of His torture upon His bloody back.

Two others were being executed with Him, but they were not so submissive about it as He. They thrashed about and cursed those who nailed them to their own cross. Burly soldiers hoisted the instruments of torture up into the air by ropes tied to their crossbeams while a man stabilized each cross from behind.

For a moment, the central cross seemed to be floating between heaven and earth for all to see.

For a moment, the central cross seemed to be floating between heaven and earth for all to see.[1] Then, suddenly and abruptly, it dropped into the hole prepared for it, landing with such a sickening thud that it seemed to shake the ground about us. The man groaned. Some of the crowd nodded approvingly;

---

1 John 19:18.

1 At the Cross

others began to weep. I tried to look away for a moment as the sun cast a blinding glare in my eyes and made sweat roll down my face and back.

Jesus hung between heaven and earth on the cross.

"Who is this man?" a stranger behind me said, repeating my question as the gawking spectators on the road shoved their way forward to see the hideous spectacle taking place. "Haven't you heard?" he said, "It is Jesus, the miracle-working carpenter and teacher from Galilee. People say that He once fed a crowd with just two fish and five loaves of bread and that He also once turned water into wine."

The sea of humanity on the road pushed me closer to the now suffering man. I saw the agony on His face as He attempted in vain to find relief by shifting His weight against the painful spikes through His flesh. Blood oozed from His back and ran down the length of the cross. I had heard about His miracles, but I did not put much stock in such stories. Whether they were real or not, I cannot say, but the suffering I was witnessing was very real.

"There's His mother," someone from the crowd pointed out as the flow of people moved closer to the place of crucifixion. A young man supported the woman, and several other women accompanied them. They had apparently stepped away from the clanging of metal on metal as soldiers pounded nails through the man's tender flesh. Yet, a mother's heart could not stay away long, and I watched as she came back to the foot of His cross.[2]

---

[2] John 19:25 says that His mother and His mother's sister, and Mary Magdalene "stood by the cross of Jesus." Yet, Luke 23:49 says that "all his acquaintance," which included Mary Magdalene and the other women (Matthew 27:55, 56; Mark 15:40), stood "afar off." That they stepped away for part of the crucifixion harmonizes the apparent discrepancy.

1 At the Cross

As she looked up, the eyes of the mother met those of her son, and everything seemed to stop—the noisy clamor of the crowd, the low whisper of the wind, and the cheerful chirping of the birds. Time itself seemed to stand still as I watched their lingering gaze, and I knew that they were having a conversation without words. He was her son; she gave Him birth.

Time itself seemed to stand still as I watched their lingering gaze, and I knew that they were having a conversation without words.

I could not help but think of my own mother and the sacrifices she made for me. How powerful is a mother's love! His mother's face was lined with pity and distress to see her baby boy suffer so. Tears had dried on her cheeks. Her eyes were swollen and red. A part of that mother was hanging on the cross, and there was nothing she could do to soothe His pain. I watched as she stood by, her tired, frail frame supported by sympathizing friends. People nearby whispered that those with the woman had been seen traveling with Jesus. The young man who held her up stood respectfully speechless by her side. I squeezed through the crowd to get closer. As hard as it was, she could not allow her son to go through this trial alone. She had supported Him in life; she would support Him now in death.

I finally reached her and realized that I had met her before. It had been in Jerusalem at the beginning of that very week—as the same man being crucified rode a donkey into the city before an adoring crowd. On that day, she had asked me what I knew about

1 At the Cross

the man who drew all eyes in the procession. I did not know Him. She told me that the man on the donkey was her son and that He had entered this world under a cloud of mystery.

"I know most mothers have visions of who and what their children can become and that they try their best to steer them in the right direction to achieve those results, but *my* son," she said as she seemed to find great delight in speaking of Him, "*my* son came into this world—and into my life—in a most unusual way, for He was given to me as a gift from God in a way that no other woman has ever experienced. I know that may sound strange to you, and, truthfully, no one I told at the time would believe me when I said that the Holy Spirit had come upon me and blessed me with a child—this child.

His Story

"I knew from the start," she said, "that His life would have a major effect on people's lives."[3] As she paused while reflecting on a pleasant memory, a smile came across her care-worn face. "Everything about Him was different," she said, "not just His conception and His birth. Even His childhood was different; one could see that He was guided by an unseen hand, a higher power."

What she told me was remarkable, and to think I heard it from the very same mother who was now watching her son die! I had looked into her eyes as she recollected memories she had treasured in her heart.[4] Now I could see a glow shining through the tears on her face as she stood by watching her beloved son hanging upon the cross.

---

3   This came from Simeon's prophecy at Jesus' dedication (Luke 2:34).
4   Luke 2:51.

1   At the Cross

She had told me about His great thirst for learning, though it seemed to her that He already knew so much. Once He learned to read, He was soon reading from the scrolls in the synagogue with great understanding and telling others about what He read. Yet, she was surprised to see Him in the temple in Jerusalem when He was twelve, debating subjects that went beyond the understanding of most boys His age. He spoke with such authority and knowledge that even adults were captivated by what He said.

At the foot of the cross, I saw the same look on her face that I had seen when she told me, "How blessed I am to have given Him birth, to have fed Him and instilled in Him the very same virtues that He Himself established for parents to teach their children. I shake my head whenever I think about giving birth to the Creator of the universe. Yet, that is who He is."

> *"I shake my head whenever I think about giving birth to the Creator of the universe."*

My thoughts came back to the present and my eyes traveled up to the man suffering before me. Why was He being crucified? Nothing that I had learned thus far gave me reason to believe that He had committed any crime deserving of such cruel punishment. My thoughts went back to my conversation with His mother.

"He was like most other children," she said. "He ran and played, and He had a smile that could brighten the darkest room. And He was always ready to help. Whatever His father or I needed Him to do He was quick to fulfill without complaint. He was—no, *is*—the perfect son."

1 At the Cross

One of the women beside her at the cross tapped me on the arm and asked me if I knew what Jesus' crime had been. Before I could tell her I did not, a voice from behind me spoke up: "He claimed to be the king of the Jews, the chosen one, the one sent to save us from our sins."[5] People around us laughed aloud at the thought.

"He doesn't look much like a king, does He?" smirked a man in fine clothes.

Then another bystander mockingly called out, "How can He save us when He can't even save Himself? Look at Him hanging there—He has no more power than you or I!"[6] A rustle of reaction rippled through the crowd.

Were these questioners right? How could He have been a miracle

---
[5]   See John 18:39; 19:21; Matthew 26:63; Luke 23:35.
[6]   See Matthew 27:42; Mark 15:31; Luke 23:35.

worker, as I had heard, if He had no power to save His own life? I could not reconcile their comments with the reality of His execution.

Finally, the woman beside me answered her own question: "Her son is hanging on that cross and giving His life because of who He is."

His mother responded, "There are far greater crimes that a mother's child could be charged with," her voice trailing off. "I am proud of my son and what He has done. His actions and beliefs define who He is and what kind of character He has." Then, with quivering lips, she added: "I know He has to do this.... I know," she hesitated, "that He has to lay down His life so God's promise can be fulfilled. But, oh, how I wish there were another way! How I wish I could die instead of my son!"

1 At the Cross

"How I wish I could die instead of my son!"

At this, she collapsed in mental exhaustion, and those around her caught her in her swoon, guiding her a short distance away to a spot where she could rest while continuing her vigil with her dying son.

This was all so much for me to consider. I could not help but replay the precious moments I had shared with the mother whose son was now being executed for claiming to be a savior and king. *"Yet, how could this be?"* I thought as I moved through the crowd to sample the reactions of others standing by. Far too many treated this event as entertainment without a care for the one being executed or for His family and friends.

As I pushed through the crowd, I heard someone shout: "If He is the Son

His Story

of God, why does He allow all of this to happen? Could He not use His powers to prove that He is the Messiah? Then I would certainly believe Him." The comment made sense. If He were indeed able to do the great things that people said He had done, why was He allowing these terrible things to happen? Some in the crowd agreed with the voice; others did not. No one knew what to expect next.

Just then I noticed some soldiers gambling at the foot of the cross. They seemed perfectly oblivious to who this man was or the good things that He had done. *"How could they be so disrespectful?"* I thought as they joined the rowdy among the Jews in taunting Jesus to come down from the cross.[7] Now these soldiers of Rome, with their disgraceful treatment of Jesus, were playing a game of chance for Jesus' few

---

7 See Matthew 27:40, 42; Mark 15:30.

1 At the Cross

personal effects. *"Have they no compassion or appreciation for the man's suffering?"* I thought. *"Maybe they are immune to the suffering of others from their repeated engagement in the crucifixion of criminals."*

The soldiers continued their gambling to see which of them would claim their blood-soaked prize. As they played, I watched and wondered what motivated them. Did they think that this man's seamless garments would fetch them a great deal of money at the auction house?[8]

I noticed one of the soldiers standing with his eyes fixed on the cross. He didn't seem interested in gambling for clothes or taunting the man for being crucified. He just stood by, gazing at the man he had helped nail to the cross. I saw the bag of nails still tied to his waist with the handle of

---

8   See John 19:23.

the hammer peering through its holder. I watched as he stared into that blood-soaked, tear-stained, sweat-filled face. As their eyes met, I saw forgiveness in Jesus' eyes as He tried to adjust His position against the effects of gravity on the nails through His feet and hands, saying, "Father, forgive them; for they know not what they do."[9]

As their eyes met, I saw forgiveness in Jesus' eyes as He tried to adjust His position against the effects of gravity on the nails through His feet and hands.

Despite His pain, Jesus was still performing an act of kindness! Was He forgiving the soldier for his part in the crucifixion? Did the soldier recognize what Jesus offered and was he giving

---

9   Luke 23:34.

1   At the Cross

his heart to the one he had just helped crucify? Mixed emotions welled up in my soul. *"How can a man love another enough to forgive him for such unjust treatment? He has to be an extraordinary person."*

I was amazed how many people stood by watching Jesus' horrible ordeal. The crowd was even larger than those that gather for important dignitaries. Yet, criminals are publicly executed all the time. So, what made this execution so different? And why was this day so uncomfortably hot? I went over to a shade tree for a little respite from the blistering heat, though still attentive to the mixed expressions of the crowd.

2

Spectators in the Crowd

Sitting in the shade, I noticed a group of young women who seemed to know Jesus, huddled together trying to comfort one another. They told me Jesus was always a gentleman and that He never treated women with disrespect. He never spoke about them in a way that made them feel cheap or unwanted.

"Even when I was caught with a man that was not my husband," one of the women said, "He didn't accuse me like everyone else. That could have been the end of me had Jesus not intervened."

Another said, "I needed acceptance, and Jesus always had a smile and a word of encouragement for me. He never took advantage of me or my feelings, and He was a good listener … a very good friend."

Her words stuck in my ears— "a very good friend."

Her words stuck in my ears— "a very good friend." My mind quickly shot back to situations in my own life in which I had the opportunity to be a friend but had responded selfishly. I had not been able to see past the moment, and my choices resulted in lasting negative effects that I will never be able to correct. I wanted what I saw at the time and had to have it. How could this man be so different from me and from most men that I know? How could He see the female form, the slenderness of a woman's neck or the dimples in her cheeks without wondering what it would be to hold and caress them? How could He smell her perfume or feel her tender touch without it triggering His desire? I needed to know what His secret was.

I overheard some people talking about seeing a man defend Jesus by lopping off the ear of one of the men who came to arrest Him. Yet, Jesus, in His humble, loving way, stopped him from doing further harm and even picked up the ear from off the ground and miraculously put it back on.

2 Spectators in the Crowd

"Can you believe that?" one of them said. "He put it back on!" I thought to myself: *"That is a little hard to believe, but does it not say something about the kindness of the man?"* He does seem like a good man—a man who does not deserve the treatment He is receiving.

As I wandered among those milling about the cross, many spoke of the great deeds that Jesus had done for the hopeless and the helpless, that He was always ready to say or to do just what was needed. Just then another voice from the crowd spoke up.

"I was once tormented by spirits that had me doing terrible things to myself and to anyone else that came around me. Yet, Jesus didn't run from me or ask me to go away. He didn't ask me why I thought I had fallen under demonic control. He simply removed the evil spirit that occupied my mind and body and gave me back a sound mind. I now have a reason for waking up in the morning, and it has been a joy just to sit at His feet listening to His lessons of love and respect for other human beings. No one has ever made me feel as loved or that I mattered as this man."

Another in the crowd told me about a man who could not walk whose friends lowered him through a hole in a roof so he could see Jesus. *"What a person to have that kind of effect on people",* I thought.

Many in the crowd seemed compelled to speak on Jesus' behalf. "We gave up everything to follow Him," one said.

"We left our homes and lucrative positions to follow Jesus," said another, "and it has never been a disappointment. Before following Jesus, I didn't understand faith, love and

2 Spectators in the Crowd

hope, but now I know why I am here and whom I belong to. I understand that no mere human being can save me, yet there has been a plan in place for that from times eternal."

"Before following Jesus, I didn't understand faith, love and hope, but now I know why I am here and whom I belong to."

I looked at the man and thought that Jesus must have made a powerful impression on people for them to leave their homes, families and livelihoods to follow Him. I wish I could have had the opportunity to talk with Jesus directly. I would have wanted to learn what set Him apart from the great orators of the day who command the attention of the masses. I would have analyzed His presentations to see how they were different from great oratory recitations.

But wasn't this man a carpenter? How could a manual laborer amass such a following? Was He just the victim of some government plot to weed out enemies of the state? Where did His authority come from and why were there so many people at the cross? Crowds of this size usually follow famous personalities and dignitaries, hoping to see or to be seen with them or, if fortunate, to receive a token of their esteem.

As I looked around, there were no banners in Jesus' support or signs demanding His release. Yet, a small group of His family, friends and followers came out to support Him. Those who claimed to have been healed by Him also came out, sharing stories of what He had done for them. Some wept uncontrollably; others sang His praises. I have never seen anything like it. There were young and old, rich

2 Spectators in the Crowd

and poor—all having had an encounter with Jesus and wanting to share what He meant to them. Eagerly I strolled about listening to their stories.

One man looked at me with beads of sweat rolling down his face and said, "They pulled me out of the crowd and thrust His cross upon my shoulders. Of all the people they could have grabbed, why did they pick me?" His question caught me off guard, but it raised a legitimate concern. "Why should I be the one to carry His cross?" he pondered. "Why should I carry the cross of a man I did not know? Who is He to me, and what have I done for this to happen to me?"

I had no answer for him. I did not know whether they saw him as a criminal or merely chose him at random or whether this was part of some greater master plan. I listened intently, looking for some hint of anger in the man's voice for being used as he was, but I never heard it. And then he totally took me by surprise. He said, "I was glad to have been there. I was glad to have the opportunity to give a part of myself to help a fellow human being. I was in the *right* place at the *right* time. I have come to believe that He is the Lamb of God." Leaving those words ringing in my ears, the man disappeared into the crowd. *"What was that?"* I thought *"—he was treated like a criminal, was used to carry another's burden, and yet the man was glad to have done it?"*

"I was in the right place at the right time. I have come to believe that He is the Lamb of God."

As I continued walking around and listening to different people, I saw a well-dressed young man sitting off

2 Spectators in the Crowd

by himself. The sadness in his eyes told me that he was distressed by what was taking place. When I asked him if he knew who Jesus was, his story tumbled out.

"I had a meeting with Jesus one day. I knew something was missing in my life, so I asked Jesus what good thing I should do to have eternal life.[10] He told me that I should keep God's commandments, and I told Him that I was already doing that. In addition, I prided myself on doing various kinds of charitable work, regularly attending synagogue, and doing other good deeds. What He told me next I was not prepared to hear. He wanted me to give everything I owned to the poor and to follow Him. Why would He ask me to do that? Didn't He know how hard I have worked to get what I have? What He asked was too much. He was telling

---

10   See Matthew 19:16.

me that I should give up my nice home and sleep outside or in a stable. He was telling me that I should give away my barns filled with livestock and food and receive the generosity of strangers. Why would it make sense for me to do that? I'm in the perfect position to help those in need. I can give money, shelter, food and clothing. No, I couldn't—I wouldn't—do what He told me to do. I've worked too hard to get what I have. What He asked wasn't fair."

With that, the man got up and walked away. I can still see the lost look in his eyes. His encounter was very different from those of others, who seemed eager to do whatever Jesus required of them, but this man had everything and yet he still seemed unhappy. It seemed as if Jesus had been unfair to him. Why should the man give up comfort in exchange for hunger and no place to call home?

2 Spectators in the Crowd

While I was thinking about this, I saw some men dressed in fine clothes with large hats surrounded by a large group of people. I recognized them as priests and rabbis and pushed my way through the crowd to talk to them. They would likely have a story to tell about Jesus, and they would surely give me the truth behind these proceedings. Maybe He had committed some hidden crime for which He was suffering.

As I came closer to the men, I noticed that they did not seem disappointed or distraught that a fellow teacher was meeting His demise. There was no look of sorrow on their faces as there was with others I had encountered. They were actually smiling as they looked at the man on the cross. These rabbis were men of God, so what pleasure could they find in one of their own being crucified? As I drew nearer, I heard one of them say how having an inside man made arresting Jesus so much easier. *"What did he mean?"* I thought. *"Surely no teacher of Israel would have entertained the thought of betraying a friend as this man Jesus had been to everyone."* I must have heard wrong. Nothing that I had heard about Him would have given me such a thought. The rabbi gloated about how easy it had been to arrest Jesus at night, with only one follower putting up resistance, and then he added: "Who did he think he was, fighting against the mob that accompanied us?"

As I drew nearer, I heard one of them say how having an inside man made arresting Jesus so much easier.

Just then another smug voice chimed in, "Thirty pieces of silver was a bargain!" I could not believe what

2 Spectators in the Crowd

I was hearing. Did these clergymen actually admit that they paid to have Jesus arrested? They must not have recognized that I was listening in.

I stepped closer to the priests and rabbis to get an explanation of this action. Powerful bodyguards stepped between me and the men they were protecting. Instantly they grabbed me and asked who I was and what I wanted. When they realized that I was unarmed, they let me through. The religious leaders spoke out without hesitation, "It's easy to see that He is guilty."

"Guilty of what?" I asked.

"Guilty of claiming to be the Son of God. Since He claims to be 'the way, the truth, and the life,' the people no longer believe that they need to bring money or livestock to us for the forgiveness of their sins.[11] In claim-

---

11   See John 14:6.

ing that there is forgiveness simply in confessing to the heavenly Father, He has insulted our "authority" and the authority of the temple. Some think He is the King of Israel, but we don't need another king.[12] Rome's rulership is enough.[13] As long as we acknowledge Rome's power, they mostly leave us alone. If we let Jesus gain popularity, we would have lost our prestige and position. Healing and helping people for free is not the way it should be done. Who would support the priests and the temple if it were all given away for free? Somebody had to stand up for the temple, and that somebody was us."

With that, they turned their backs to me and continued their conversation with one another. I could not believe what I had just heard: Jesus, the man being crucified, was condemned for doing what God's

12 See John 12:13.
13 See John 19:15.

2 Spectators in the Crowd

people were supposed to do, except that He did it for free. The leaders could not tolerate His directing the people to humbly ask the heavenly Father for forgiveness and receive it for free.

"When and where is it fair, or even legal, to condemn someone for that?" I thought. *"How can an innocent man be put through all of this for pointing people to a God who saves?"*

Just then, I noticed a smaller group of rabbis who had not joined in the reveling of their peers in their victory over Jesus. I could see that their eyes were filled with tears, though they avoided making eye contact. That set off alarms in my head. *"It is a sure sign of guilt when a person cannot look another in the eye,"* I thought remembering a lesson I had learned as a child. It was always hard for me to look my parents in the eye when I had done something wrong. I felt that they must know what I had done already. Yet, slow to learn, I would lie to cover it up, not realizing that my eyes gave me away. Did these men's downward glance indicate that they were hiding something they really wanted to say?

As the main group of priests and rabbis walked away slapping each other on the back, I made my way over to those who were left behind to ask them face to face what they thought about what was taking place. I was hoping to hear the deeper truth that their peers had been unwilling to share. With heads bowed low and voices shaking, they told me, "We made a huge mistake. We were part of a plot to do away with a man we now believe to have been who He claimed to be. We manipulated the people; we conspired with the Roman authorities to arrest and crucify Jesus the Christ. We even paid one of His followers to hand Him over

2 Spectators in the Crowd

to us. We rushed Him through night court under false accusations. We had Him beaten, and now we are watching Him being put to death. All of this is happening because He simply told the truth—the truth about Himself, about His power and about the condition of the human heart. Now it's too late for us to stop what we got started."

All of this is happening because He simply told the truth—the truth about Himself, about His power and about the condition of the human heart.

With bitterness of heart, they told me about the insider they had employed in carrying out their secret plot. They also told me how this same insider and follower of Jesus broke into the council chamber, screaming, "He is innocent! Spare Him, O Caiaphas! He has done nothing worthy of death!"[14] And then he threw down before the high priest the money he received for Jesus' betrayal.

At first, this took the whole council off guard. However, when the high priest had regained his composure, he coldly sent the man away under the hissing of the council. With a horrible look of remorse on his face, the man went out and hung himself. The thought of that pathetic man hanging from a tree burned an image in my mind that I would not soon forget.

It was becoming clearer to me that Jesus was not guilty of anything but loving and teaching others to do the same. How could such a miscarriage of justice be allowed? We are a civilized, enlightened people. Many of us possess a classical Greek education. Yet, here we are today, taking a barbaric leap backward.

---

14   Ellen G. White, *The Desire of Ages*, p. 721.

2 Spectators in the Crowd

My curiosity about the proceedings of the day had by now turned into compassion for a man who had only done good things for other human beings—the same human beings who clamored for His death.

3

A Shift in the Weather

The sun was fading away now, and the breath-taking heat has been replaced by gusts of wind, like those just before a hurricane blast. *"When did the weather change?"* I thought to myself. I had been so immersed in the

3 A Shift in the Weather

scenes taking place before me that I had no time to notice the elements.

I had spent what has seemed like hours walking and talking with people in the crowd. I had heard from everyone, it seems, except the crucified man who people said was dying for those who were crucifying Him. I wanted to talk with Him, but it was now too late. I had not spent time with Him when He walked the streets and hillsides preaching and teaching. There had been no interview with the condemned as He ate His last meal. How could I in good conscience interview a man while He was dying?

The sun was all but gone; only a glimmer of it appeared behind the clouds.

The sun was all but gone; only a glimmer of it appeared behind the clouds. The air smelled of rain as storm clouds began to roll in. *"Where was the sunshine that had shown so brightly just a few hours ago? Where did all this wind come from?"*

Having seen enough, some people started to leave. Little groups of people huddled together as they made their way from the scene of the crucifixion. Some huddled for protection from the howling winds and the pelting sting of the rain. Others huddled for the support they needed as they were mourning the loss of a friend. Some went away with the same frame of mind they had when they first arrived. Others entertained new thoughts, inspired by some unseen force they had never felt before. Besides these, there were others, like myself, who stayed behind, either because they did not want to miss anything or simply because they could not let go. Which it was for me at

3 A Shift in the Weather

the time is hard to say, for I was torn between curiosity and a mysterious change that was taking place in my thoughts and feelings. I do not think that it was merely the emotion of the moment. Something real and different was happening in me, and it felt good. It felt right. I felt a connection that I had never felt before. Yet, I was also experiencing a terrible loss, a sense of regret and a growing void that I wondered if I could ever fill. The one on the cross was someone I had never met before and undoubtedly would never see again. How could I have such an emotional attachment to Him?

Everyone knew that something momentous was taking place.

As the winds picked up, black, angry clouds rolled in and heavy raindrops began to fall. The sunshine

His Story

of the day had been taken over by a shroud of darkness, engulfing the place of crucifixion in the city. Yet, it was still early. It was as if the elements above were showing their sadness for what was happening. Everyone knew that something momentous was taking place. Just as this strange weather crept in, I heard one of the other men hanging beside Jesus painfully call out to Him, "If You are the Son of God, save Yourself and us."[15] Immediately, another voice broke through the howl of the wind. It was that of the man hanging on the other side of Jesus.

"Hold your tongue, Gestas! We are guilty of our crimes and deserve our punishment. But, this man has done nothing worthy of death."[16]

---

15   See Luke 23:39.
16   See Luke 23:41. The name "Gestas" comes from the apocryphal Gospel of Nicodemus. No one knows for sure what his name actually was.

3 A Shift in the Weather

It was hard for me to believe what I was hearing—a criminal speaking up for someone else dying with him, testifying to the other's goodness. The man knew that he and his fellow criminal were guilty of their crimes, but he did not understand why this horrible thing was happening to such a good man as Jesus. He paused as he struggled for breath. Pain was taking over—every breath was a struggle, and every movement caused extreme pain. I stood by and watched as he tried to use his final moments to ask for forgiveness. He asked forgiveness for the life he had wasted and for those he had wronged. He asked to be remembered when Jesus entered His kingdom. It was amazing to see this criminal's transformation and his willingness to put his trust in one who was seemingly as vulnerable as he. Yet, what was more amazing was the response that Jesus offered him back.

Despite His own agony and weakness, Jesus summoned enough strength to lift up His head. The two men looked eye to eye, and soul bonded to soul in that moment. With a voice of compassion and authority, Jesus said, "Truly to you I say this day, you will be with Me in Paradise."[17] The man needed to hear nothing else. Those few words said it all. The man recognized in Jesus a friend, a brother and a Savior. Jesus recognized in the man a friend, a brother and a lost soul who had been found.

The two men looked eye to eye, and soul bonded to soul in that moment.

In realizing that time was running out for Jesus as He hung on the cross, I knew that my time was also short. I did not yet understand why He

---

17   Luke 23:43, literal translation of the Greek.

3 A Shift in the Weather

was willing to die. What purpose was so great that He would be willing to give His life? I needed to talk to Him before it was too late.

As I pushed my way through the small group of people still gathered around the cross, I stumbled and fell to my knees. As I fell, my eyes, for some reason, quickly glanced upward. I saw His face; I saw His pain. I needed to talk with Him, but all I could do was stay on my knees and look up. At that very instant, I saw Him shift His weight to find some relief from His pain, and drops of blood fell from His brow, splashing on my head and running down my face. I now had Jesus' blood on me, and it dawned on me that blood was a symbol of life and of the forgiveness of sins in the sacrifices in the temple. Like the rest of the people who had witnessed His crucifixion, I would never be the same again. We had seen and been a part of something strange and different, weather changing, and—yes—life changing.

He groaned as He fought to balance Himself between heaven and earth, between good and evil, between what was and what was to come, between life and death. I had wanted to talk with Him, but my time was now passed, and His time was almost over. I had wasted too much time talking to others. I had allowed my enthrallment with their stories to keep me away from His.

Just as I was beginning to feel sorry for myself, I felt a touch on my shoulder, and a calm voice said to me, "In time, you will understand all this, and you will be able to share your story with others." I wondered how I heard the voice so clearly with the wind blowing, the rain falling, and the people around the cross crying and moaning.

4

"It Is Finished"

My thoughts were all a blur. Before I could respond to the voice behind me, I heard Jesus cry out in agony, "My God! My God! why have You abandoned Me?"[18] Was He really talking to God in heaven? It surely felt like it! Then, almost immediately, He called out, "Father, 'into your hands I

---

18   See Matthew 27:46; Mark 15:34.

commit My spirit!' It ... is finished!"[19] And then He bowed His head and died.

"It ... is finished!"

"No! No!" I shouted, bowing my own head, partly because I was angry that I had not discovered why He would let Himself be killed but partly because I felt something happening inside me. I was feeling that I had lost someone special to me. *"No, it can't be over,"* I thought. *"Not yet! I need more time! I never had the chance to talk to Him!'*

Again the voice spoke to me and said, "This is why you are here. See where you are? You are at the foot of the cross with your head bowed before Jesus, sprinkled with the blood of the Creator of the universe, the King, the Son of the living God.[20] He did all this to

---

19   Luke 23:46, NKJV; John 19:30.
20   See Matthew 16:16; John 6:69.

forgive your sins! He knew that one day you would be searching for answers. He knew that one day you would realize how important He is and how much you need Him in your life. He knew that one day you would write a story—not one that would soon be forgotten but one that would endure and that would encourage others to evaluate their own life. He knew that you would write a story about a man who gave His life even though He had all power in heaven and earth, a man who stood in the gap between heaven and hell, between life and death. He also knew that you would be a single parent, that you would struggle with addictions and that illness would alter your body and mind. He knew that the devil would fight to get control of you and that he would try even harder to kill you. He did this for you and for everyone like you who would receive the gift. All you need to do is reach up and accept the gift—the gift of eternal life."

As I tried to compose myself, I managed to look up at Jesus on the cross through the wind, rain and darkness that covered us. I then understood why I was attracted to the cross. I knew that there had been a void in my life and that I was searching for something. I had become disconnected from that which I had been taught as a child, like praying and studying God's Word and being kind to those who were unkind to me. Work, family and the everyday business of life had crowded out any quiet time with God. I had become impatient, unloving and unkind. I now understood that I was here at the cross—not just to satisfy curiosity but to accept the gift—the gift that had been freely given, though purchased with pain and suffering. I was witnessing the love, grace and mercy that are offered to all, and

4 "It Is Finished"

I was to share what I was witnessing with others. I could not keep these to myself. Despite my sudden and unexpected inspiration, I still could not help but wonder: Was there not a happier end to this man's story?

I watched as the soldiers lowered His body from the cross. Most of the crowd had already dispersed, yet some still lingered, perhaps waiting to see if He would get up in one last grand miracle, fulfilling the prediction that He would rise again.[21]

I stood to my feet, motionless, with tears streaming down my face. I thought about my life and how it was time for me to make a change. I did not want to be the same. There was no way I was going to allow all I had seen slip by without its changing me, and I felt a desire to share what had happened to me with others. I wanted

---

21   See Jesus' prediction in Mark 8:31.

to find a place to gather my thoughts. Yet, something or someone was holding me where I was.

The soldiers' grim work was done. Those who cheered His death had gotten what they wanted. He was dead; He was gone. Yet, I just stood there, looking at the now empty cross illumined by the light of a nearby bonfire. His bloodied, limp body was no longer on the cross.

Two well-dressed men received Jesus' body from the soldiers and carefully loaded it onto a wagon to be cleaned up and prepared for burial. I watched as the little group proceeded down the way with the body of Jesus. A small number of mourners followed. This included Jesus' mother, His closest followers and a few others who just could not let go. Soldiers also stood by, commissioned to keep a watchful eye on the body of Jesus to ensure that His followers did not try to steal it to make it appear that His bold prediction that He would rise from the dead after three days had been fulfilled.

He would rise from the dead after three days had been fulfilled.

    I followed the little procession, curious of what would come next and not wanting to be by myself. I wanted to be with the people who had spent time living and traveling with Him. I wanted—no, *needed*—to be part of their group, for I still had so many questions that they might be able to answer. As we made our way toward the place of burial, I thought I would tell the little group how privileged I felt to have been at the cross with them. I also wanted to share with them about the voice that told me that this had happened for me—that it had happened for us. When I did, I found that others had similar thoughts.

As His body was placed in the tomb, we consoled each other and found a place a stone's throw away to sit and watch the soldiers seal the tomb and take their post of duty. I took a spot close to a fire as the sun was disappearing completely from view.

5

At Rest

I felt comfortable among these people. I could see among them no attitude of superiority nor competition about who it was that Jesus had loved or blessed the most. We were just a band of people brought together by circumstance, and now we had a story to tell and a bond between us, though we came from different walks of life. Yet, I was also aware that there was reason to fear the authorities. If they could crucify Jesus, what might they do to those who followed Him?

Yet, strangely, I was at peace. As we settled in for the night, I could hardly rest because I kept thinking about what would happen next. However, to my surprise, I soon drifted off to sleep. It was a peaceful rest for me—unlike I had had for a very long time.

I awakened the next morning to see many of those who had fallen asleep around me already up and stirring. What were they doing? Ah, of course! It was Sabbath—God's holy day of rest, set apart by God's command, when we would normally be praying and studying the Scriptures

5 At Rest

in the synagogue.[22] I found it strange that, despite their caution about the religious leaders, the group was still intent on the joyful experience of worship. How could they be cheerful at all when their friend, companion and loved one had just been killed and laid to rest? At the service, they could not keep from talking about Jesus and His encouraging words—His command to love those who treat us wrong and to serve God and our fellow human beings. They spoke about turning the other cheek and treating others as we would want to be treated.

As I listened, I was transported back to a time when I wasn't so quick to get angry and I chose my words

---

22   Luke wrote that they "rested the sabbath day according to the commandment" (Luke 23:56). Luke mentioned that, even years after the crucifixion, Paul looked for a place on the Sabbath where "prayer was wont to be made" and that he reasoned on several Sabbaths "out of the scriptures" (Acts 16:13; 17:2).

more carefully. Back then, work was more enjoyable and people were more comfortable opening up to me. Maybe there was something to this attitude toward others that Jesus taught. I wanted what these people had.

After the service, we shared a simple meal and talked more about the goodness of our friend who had been slain. Yes, I did call Him "friend," for I also felt a special kinship with Him. We did our best to take comfort in our great loss through psalms and prayers.

His mother was there too. She encouraged us to be strong and to believe the words that her son had spoken. "All is not lost," she said, "His words are not only kind, but they are true."

I thought to myself, *"What a strong, proud and loving mother she is!"* She could have left us to grieve

5 At Rest

alone, but she wanted to stay with us to give and receive comfort. I felt that I belonged with them. I felt a spirit of power with this group. Was this not the way that fellowship is supposed to feel? Was it not an attitude of friendship, love and honesty?

I made up my mind right then that it was time that I go back home and make some things right and then return to assist Jesus' followers in their work of ministry to others in greater need than they. I voiced my plans to one of them, and he said to me: "You don't have to wait until later. You can begin right now." I was stunned, but the man explained, "I am not talking about giving away your clothes or your money. I am talking about sharing your experience. You would be surprised how a person's testimony can affect others who have gone through a similar experience."

Now, I have only occasionally spoken in religious service, but I thought, *"These people have been so kind to me, and I now feel a sense of liberation from the old me. Why not give it a chance?"* So I did. I began to tell those gathered how I had been drawn to Jesus out of curiosity but that something had taken hold of me, keeping me from leaving.

I began to tell those gathered how I had been drawn to Jesus out of curiosity but that something had taken hold of me, keeping me from leaving.

"It's funny," I said. "The very same things my parents tried to instill in me have been in the back of my mind all this time pricking my conscience whenever I did something wrong. Now

5 At Rest

I feel a sense of relief. The pressure to outwit and outdo others is no longer vying for control. I now have a desire to be truthful and honest in everything I do."

My words seemed to touch some of those present, for I could see in their faces a look of relief. It felt good to be a part of something that was important, something that was right, something that changed lives. Like me, these new believers were ready to join the movement, to spread the good news of Jesus the Christ. I had never experienced such a reaction.

Who was I becoming? What was next for me? I liked this new me. I felt a hunger to learn more about Jesus and His life. My questions were now more of a personal nature. As the day passed, I could not help but feel anxious about what would happen next.

6

The Night Vigil

I decided to make my way back that night to the tomb where I found the soldiers still posted. They looked tired but still formidable. I wondered if they understood what had taken place and if it had made any change in their heart. I could not imagine that anyone could witness all that we had seen without it having some effect.

6 The Night Vigil

I was a bit surprised that the soldiers were the only ones waiting at the garden tomb. Did Jesus' followers not believe that He would rise again or were they past their loss and ready to move on? Whatever they felt, I was not going to miss out on what came next.

I joined people gathered around a fire, telling stories of what Jesus had done in healing their illnesses and in speaking words of encouragement to them. I met a woman who said that she had been sick for a long time but that she had been fortunate enough to touch the hem of Jesus' robe and that was enough to do for her what many doctors had been unable to do. She started crying, overwhelmed with joy—not merely because of her physical healing but because she had felt true compassion that she had not felt for years, having been a social outcast because of her illness. She paused as she gathered her thoughts and, with a sigh, she bowed her head and offered a prayer of thanksgiving for the love of Jesus and of petition for the group to know what our mission should be. "His death cannot be in vain," she said. "There are many who will need to hear this story, and it is our responsibility to pass it on." I was reflecting on what she said when another began sharing her experience.

"I was caught with another woman's husband. Guilty of sin, I was dragged out into the center of town and about to be stoned by my accusers. Just then Jesus stooped down and started writing in the sand on the pavement and then proclaimed, 'He that is without sin cast the first stone.' I did not look up, but one by one I could hear those gathered to take my life, turn and walk away. I have no idea what Jesus wrote," she said pausing, "but He saved

6   The Night Vigil

my life that day. What amazes me is that, in the middle of all the commotion, He remained calm, though speaking with authority. He looked down at me as I lay on the ground where the townspeople had thrown me, and He reached out His hand. I can remember the gentleness of His touch as He lifted me to my feet with a power that I had never felt from a man's hand before. He asked me where the men were who had accused me. But they were gone—every one of them! Even the crowd that had gathered had moved on, and it was just He and I standing there. At that moment, I knew I was changed. The life I had previously led was over. I would never be the same."

I heard story after story as we sat there through the night, enjoying each other's company and reflecting on what Jesus had done for each one. Though I had expected a few of Jesus' closest followers to be there, I did not expect to see the soldier who nailed Him to the cross. I remembered the look that he and Jesus had exchanged. Now he found himself linked to Jesus—the man who had done so much for so many and who was now lying dead in a tomb, behind a large stone, guarded by Roman soldiers.

Though I had expected a few of Jesus' closest followers to be there, I did not expect to see the soldier who nailed Him to the cross.

I looked at this man I had seen at the cross. I watched him as he found a spot away from the larger groups and his fellow soldiers. His weather-beaten face told of a rough life, and his imposing stature made me think twice about approaching him. I watched as a tear rolled down his face. "I helped kill Him," he wept aloud, "I heard the false accusations and joined in with the rabble's taunts. I was there, and I did nothing to stop it. Rather, I lifted Him up when they knocked Him down, and I pushed Him forward when He had no more energy to go on. I pulled the man from the crowd to carry His cross, and "*I nailed Jesus to the cross*," he said, rising to his feet. "How could I have been so blind? I felt inside me that the whole affair was wrong. Yet, I did what I was told to do, as a good soldier does."

Standing just a few feet from this formidable soldier, I was at a loss for words. He continued in a broken tone, "I am so sorry for being a part of this travesty of justice in executing an innocent man. Please pray for me," he said, "and for the other soldiers that they too can repent of what they have done." I was surprised that this seasoned soldier had feelings like the rest of us and that he had a guilty conscience for what he had done. He needed to know that he and his fellow soldiers could be forgiven. He needed to be reminded of Jesus' words, "Father, forgive them, for they known not what they do."

I looked up at the stars trying to name the different constellations to keep from falling asleep. I was caught up thinking about what the next day would bring. It would be the "third day." If Jesus' prediction were indeed true, I wanted to be awake to see it all.

The night sky was clear and bright. The moon was full, and its light gave me a feeling of comfort. For the first time in a long time, my mind was clear, and my thoughts weren't scattered. I had found calm in my soul. The night air was crisp and slightly

6   The Night Vigil

cool. I noticed a few clouds rolling in, but it did not feel like rain. As the fires died down, I decided to get a little sleep near the tomb just in case something should happen.

7

The Dawn's Early Light

A sudden flash of light and the shaking of the earth, which felt as if a huge boulder had dropped from the sky and crashed into the ground, cut short my peaceful rest. The burst of light was so bright that I could see it with my eyes closed.

7 The Dawn's Early Light

"Are we under attack?" I thought as I stirred from my slumber. *"But who would want to attack a cemetery? That would not make sense."*

Something had happened, yet we did not know what it was. The soldiers who had been dispatched to watch over the tomb were picking themselves up from the ground where they had been knocked down by an invisible force. Someone called out, "Look, the stone at the entrance of the tomb has been moved!"

How was this possible? Who could have done this thing while we were sleeping and the Roman guard was keeping watch? For a moment, I stood speechless. Had Jesus come back to life? I needed to see for myself. Was this man's death the end, or had His words come true?

Gathering my courage, I approached the open tomb. The hardened soldiers looked perplexed. They were examining the broken seal on the tomb with worried looks. They most certainly knew what would happen to them for allowing the violation of the tomb.

My pulse quickened as I looked into the tomb and saw what the guards had seen before me—the tomb was now empty, and the body was nowhere to be found! *"Had it really happened? I thought—had Jesus really come back from the grave?"*

I stood frozen in my thoughts as others came one by one to see the now empty tomb. People began to cry, assuming that, while we slept, someone had come and taken Jesus' body away. But how could that have happened? I was awake most of the night and the only noise we heard was the loud crashing sound with the burst of light. There was no way that anyone

7 The Dawn's Early Light

could have gotten past the soldiers to move the stone and slip into the tomb and remove Jesus' body. Besides, who would dare break Pilate's seal?

Shouts of fear and amazement filled the morning air. *"The body is gone,"* I thought as I stood by with my hands on my head. The room that once held Jesus' body is empty except for His burial covering, which was folded and placed neatly where His body once lay. Something inside me wanted to believe that it was true, that He was risen from the dead, but it was just too incredible!

As I turned and walked out of the tomb, I noticed that the scene had changed.

As I turned and walked out of the tomb, I noticed that the scene had changed. The sounds of crying and the scurrying of the soldiers looking for the body or evidence of intruders to help them prove that they had not failed in their responsibility were now replaced with silence as every eye was fixed just above the tomb. What were they all looking at? Turning and looking up, I saw what they saw, a man sitting on the rocks above the tomb. His face glowed with a radiant light. With wide eyes, we watched as he stood and spoke:

"I was dispatched from the God of heaven to come down and remove the stone that was put in place to hold the body of Jesus. Do not worry or be afraid, for death and the grave have been conquered. Jesus is alive!"

"He's alive!" I thought as I looked at the others who stood transfixed on the figure delivering this amazing news.

"Jesus has risen from the dead," he continued. "Go tell His followers that He is alive."

I so wanted to believe that Jesus had defeated death, but I could not be

7 The Dawn's Early Light

sure. Some of the ones who had been at the empty tomb went running to town to tell what they had just heard and seen. I stood by for a moment and then took one last look at the tomb. The vault that once held the man who had predicted that death could not hold Him was the place of new life for me, of new joy and of new friends. Not far from where I was standing I noticed a figure beneath a tree, who also glowed with radiant light. Something about him drew me to him. As I came close, he reached out his hand and placed it on my shoulder. His touch felt familiar. It was what I had felt while on my knees at the foot of the cross. As he spoke, I listened carefully.

"Do not worry," He said. "Jesus is alive. You will yet see Him and talk with Him. Jesus is eager to share some things with you. Everything will be all right, for the heavenly Father is in control of all things. You were meant to be here to see and write about it. You have been chosen to be one of His. You have endured hard times and have held on. You spent years on the other side, but now you know the price that Jesus paid to redeem the lives of those who love Him. You have been blessed because Jesus did this for you and for everyone who will believe in Him. Go now, tell His followers and friends what you have seen."

And then he vanished, and I found myself standing there alone. The soldiers had run off to work out a deal with the religious leaders to protect their lives. The crowd had run off to tell what they had observed. I knew that I too had something to say. I had satisfied my curiosity about who Jesus was, but now I was curious to know what message He had for me. Maybe His followers could explain what I had seen and heard.

8

In the Upper Room

I learned at the tomb where His friends could be found in the upper room of a house in Jerusalem. Some of them had been there since His crucifixion and burial, trying to stay out of sight. After having been with Jesus and having heard His words of life and seen His miracles, it must have been hard for them not to have Him with them. They must have felt alone and afraid. Their leader had been executed, and they could be next.

The mood in the room was somber. Those who were gathered shared in their feelings of loss. That Jesus had told them He was going to be rejected and killed did not remove their pain. How could they now go on? Where should they go? Should they continue living according to His teachings or should they all just go their separate ways, thankful that they had been blessed with time with Jesus?

The news of Jesus' empty tomb and the angel's message spread quickly through the streets, and now the message had finally reached His closest disciples. The first bearer of the good news was a woman.

8 In the Upper Room

"I have seen Him. I have seen Him!"

"I have seen Him. I have seen Him!" she blurted as she entered the room. "He's alive!" She was full of joy as she told of her meeting with the Master. She told how she had gone to the garden and found the tomb empty except for Jesus' burial clothes. She was startled to find two men sitting inside the tomb—one at the head and the other at the feet where Jesus' body had been.[23] One of the men asked her why she was crying. In her sorrow, she said, "Because they have taken away my Lord, and I don't know where they have put Him."[24] Then she saw another man, believing Him to be a caretaker of the cemetery garden.

---

23   See John 20:12.
24   John 20:13.

She paused, trying to maintain her composure. "I walked over to where the man was. Through my tears, I asked where they had taken my master. The man spoke my name, "Mary," and said: 'It is I. I am here.' I looked," she said, "and it was Jesus. He is alive! He told me to come and tell you that He would come to us, and that is why I am here. It is because He is coming."

Her announcement brought much-needed relief to the room. "*Maybe His prediction is true,*" I thought. "*Maybe He has come back from the dead.*" Speculation buzzed around the room. Other women arrived and told of their seeing Jesus too. One in the room repeated Jesus' words about His returning in three days. Some considered the announcement of His resurrection "idle tales."[25] Others were

---

25   Luke 24:11.

8   In the Upper Room

simply still trying to come to grips with the fact that Jesus was no longer with them. Before I could invite myself into the conversation, a man spoke up from the corner of the room.

"He healed me," he said, pausing to let his words sink in. "I was crippled, and my friends thought it would help if I came to see the great healer. They were so sure that He would help me that they picked me up in my bed and carried me to where Jesus was speaking. When we arrived at the house, the crowd was so thick that we could not get in. Yet, because of the faith of my friends, failure was not an option. They decided that, if we couldn't get to Jesus through the door, we would get to Him through the roof. No matter what it took, they were going to get me to the man they believed would heal me. Breaking through the roof, they lowered me down in front of Jesus.

Imagine what the people in that house must have thought in seeing my bed coming out of the ceiling in a sudden shaft of dusty light! That day Jesus healed me—not because of my faith or because of some great thing that I had done but because of the faith of my friends. And I am here today to give honor and praise to the one who gave me new life."

The man looked around the room and asked, "How can you question whether Jesus' words are true? How can you question if He has risen from the dead? Seeing all that He did for so many, how can you let your faith be shaken? If He said it, that should be enough for any of us."

Jesus' followers looked at the man as he spoke to them. They knew that he was right. The disciples had been part of a great movement that Jesus called "the kingdom of Heaven."

8 In the Upper Room

They had been with Jesus when He raised the dead, when He healed the sick and when He fed the hungry. They had seen His miracles and His blessings first hand, and they should have known better. They should have known that, if Jesus could do such great miracles, there was nothing beyond His reach. They received the man's admonition with tears of joy, which counteracted to a large part the sorrow in their heart, and they thanked him for his encouragement. The shadow of gloom in the room continued to lift.

As the day wore on, more reports of the risen Master were delivered to the residents of the upper room. The same room that was once quiet and sad slowly began filling with infectious excitement. Once again, just as around the tomb on Sabbath eve, people swapped stories about the goodness of Jesus and what He had done for them.

His Story

There was a young girl in the room with her family who had been raised from her deathbed. Now she was full of life and joy, and her face glowed with the happiness of the gift of life that Jesus had given her. Her mother and father said that there was nothing that could change their minds about Jesus and His love. "His words gave us back our child, and we will trust in Him forever," they said. The mood in the room was now so much brighter than what it had been, and it was about to get brighter still.

The disciples opened the door and in stumbled two out-of-breath men. They greeted one as "Cleopas." At the same time, I noticed a loan figure moving through the room, seemingly unnoticed. He found a spot at one of the tables and sat down. I watched Him look around at those gathered in the room. "*Who is this*

8 In the Upper Room

man?" I thought. He looked familiar, but his hood shadowing his eyes kept me from getting a good look at His face. Yet, I felt I knew Him.

The two who had just entered told the amazing story of walking with Jesus on the road to Emmaus, a village about eight miles from Jerusalem. They told us, however, that they did not recognize Jesus when He first approached them and asked them about why they looked so sad. Ironically, they responded by asking Him if He had not heard about the things that had recently transpired there. Not breaking a smile, Jesus, who was to them a stranger, asked, "What things?" And then they told Him about Jesus of Nazareth, His great works for the people, and His condemnation by the Jewish rulers and subsequent crucifixion. Then they said disappointedly, "But we were hoping that it was He who was going to redeem Israel. Indeed, besides all this, today is the third day since these things happened."[26] They also told the stranger about the women's report that the tomb was empty and about the women's conversation with angel messengers. The stranger reprimanded them for their slowness of belief, and He showed them in the Scriptures how the Messiah was supposed to suffer and die. Then, the men told how they recognized, as they sat down to eat and He blessed their food, that the stranger was Jesus. At that instant, He vanished, and they took off running in the dark to Jerusalem to deliver their good news.

Their story sparked "amens" from several in the room, though some still maintained a quiet reserve. The anticipation of Jesus' arrival could hardly be contained. I must admit that

---

26 Luke 24:21, NKJV.

my own heart was beating faster. I wanted to see Him and talk with Him.

Just then, the mystery man stood up. He had entered the room without notice, but now every eye was fastened on Him. In a voice that all recognized, He said, "Peace be unto you." It was Jesus. He was with us! His words cushioned the shock of seeing Him alive. He showed us the wounds from the nails in His hands and feet. "It is I," He said.

In a voice that all recognized, He said, "Peace be unto you."

Jesus had returned to us—just as He said He would! Cries of joy and praise filled the room. The prophecy was true! Everyone wanted to thank Jesus personally and to praise and touch Him. I found it hard to contain my own joy. Yet, I still wanted to have my turn with Him.

After Jesus had greeted each disciple individually, He addressed the entire group, saying, "I will be leaving this world and going to My Father's house. I want you to continue to preach, teach and heal. I want you to share the gospel of our heavenly Father with all you meet. I want you to know My joy and peace. There is still much work to do. It will not be easy, yet you will not be alone. I will send you one to be at your side—the Holy Spirit. He will sustain you in carrying on this work."[27]

---

27 Jesus referred to the Holy Spirit as another "comforter" (John 14:16), which is *paraklētos* in Greek, meaning "one called to the side of."

9

A Personal Interview

As Jesus moved through the crowd, He stopped by me. This was amazing—Jesus was standing next to me! He said:

"I understand that you have some questions for Me. Let Me see if I can give you the answers you seek.

My life and death were predetermined from the beginning of time. When sin entered planet Earth, the plan was put into effect.

"I knew you before you were even a thought in your parents' mind. I watched you grow. I was with you when your father died and you felt lost. I was with you holding things together when you had no idea where to turn. I have carried you through the times you have thought you were all alone and no one cared for you. I watched over your family and kept the evil one from taking complete control over your lives. You did not know it, but it was I who breathed life back into your body when the doctors had lost all hope. It was I who gave you back your mind when the devil tried to take it from you. I have given you the strength to work and to move when others have had to take a seat. I heard your prayers when

9 A Personal Interview

you asked why you had to go through difficulties—sickness, struggles, and loneliness.

"What you did not see was that I had My arms around you, holding and protecting you. Yes, I allowed trials to come into your life, but that was because I knew the plan I had for you and I had confidence in you. I heard you cry out that you weren't Job and that it was too much for you. I sent people into your life—some just for a season—to comfort you when you tried to close your ears to My voice. I know what you are made of and that is why I was willing to put you through the fire to prove to you and to the world that I am who I say I am and that you are My child.

"My hand has been on you since you took your first breath. I needed you to experience hard times so you could appreciate good ones. You needed to experience loss so you could help others who suffer as you did. Your body had to be afflicted so you would be able to identify with others who are sick. Your family had to be touched so you would learn the meaning of compassion, love and grace. I did this to you because I knew that I had equipped you with everything that you needed to come through it.

"And now I am asking to use you again. Let your light shine; let your life be put on display.[28] Allow others to know all that I have done for you. Through you, others will learn of Me and of My goodness and love for them. You may not preach a sermon, but your life will be a testimony of what I am able to do. Allow Me to work through you, and watch what I can do."

I listened with tears in my eyes, remembering the events that He had

---

28   See Matthew 5:16.

9 A Personal Interview

described. I remembered being in situations with no way out and seeing doors open that I could not have expected. I remembered losing my mind only for it to return the very same day. I remembered the pain of surgeries and coming back from them stronger. I remembered hearing that my life was a testimony to others but not believing that it could be so. I remembered thinking that God and Jesus must not be concerned with my struggles. I remembered crying, asking for it all to be over, and now it all made sense. My trials had come to make me strong. The "me" that once was, has changed. I finally understand my purpose. I finally understand why I had to go through trials. It wasn't just for me; it wasn't just because I had a lesson to learn. It was to make me the man God wanted me to be and because people would be watching. I had been held up before Satan whom God asked, "Have you considered My servant, Robert?"[29]

All that Jesus revealed to me was a bit overwhelming. I needed to sit down. When I did, Jesus put His hand on my shoulder and told me not to let the story end here but to write down what I had learned, what I had seen and what He has said. "I will use you to help others," He said. "The enemy will try to harm you, but you are Mine, and I have already prepared a place for you in My kingdom.[30] You will fall, but, rest assured, I will pick you up again.[31] Times may be lean, but I promise to take care of your needs.[32] People will walk away from you and mistreat you, but I will give you a spirit of forgiveness, and you will use those difficult times to fuel the fire of your heart to

---

29 Compare Job 1:8; 2:3.
30 See John 14:1–3.
31 See Proverbs 24:16.
32 See Psalm 37:25.

9   A Personal Interview

work even harder for Me. The war that will rage around you will not require you to fight but only to remain standing. I will guide your footsteps, and those who bless you, I will bless; those who curse you, I will curse.[33] Your life will be a living testimony of what I can do. Just keep your hand in Mine. Then, when it's all said and done, you will hear, 'Well done good and faithful servant; enter into My Father's house.' "[34]

I listened to His words and recognized the task Jesus had for me. I was afraid and hopeful at the same time. I determined that I wanted to hear in the end His words, "Well done, My servant." My life would never be the same, for now, I knew my purpose. I had gotten *His* story, and, in the process, I had gotten *my* story as well. I had heard from Jesus Himself that my

---

33   See Genesis 12:3, the promise to Abraham and his spiritual seed.

34   Adapted from Matthew 25:23.

trials had come to make me strong. I had heard from Jesus Himself that I matter to Him and that all things have been in His hands.

Then Jesus asked me if He could ask me a question. It was hard enough that the King of kings, the Creator of the universe, who was born among men, predicted His owns death and then died and rose again was now standing beside me, but to have Him ask if He could ask me a question was truly humbling.

Recognizing who He is, I had no other choice but to say, "Speak, Lord," and then I waited wondering if He was going to ask me about things I had done in my past—things that I had done under the cover of darkness, things I thought no one else knew. I wondered if He would ask me about my having taken things that did not belong to me. I wondered if He would

9 A Personal Interview

ask about the deep, dark secret that I had been holding inside, which made me the way I was. I did not know what He would ask, but I knew that, whatever it was, I could not lie, for He already knew the truth.

My palms were sweating, my knees were shaking and my throat was painfully dry. My heart was pounding and my breathing shallow, waiting for the question that Jesus had for me. I tried to clear my mind of all of the thoughts that were swirling around for I knew that He could see them all. Perhaps I could make my mind go blank so that He would not see what was in me. No, that made no sense. He knows me inside and out.

"Don't be a coward," I told myself. *"Whatever it is, He already knows about it and has shed His blood for it to be forgiven. Calm down and learn from the experience."* After minutes

seemed to have passed, I told Jesus in my deepest and most confident voice: "You can ask me anything."

> *With His deepest and kindest voice, He asked me: "Do you love Me?"*

Then, with His deepest and kindest voice, He asked me: "Do you love Me?"[35] I looked up and said, "With all that You have done for me, how could I *not* love You?" He smiled at me, and I knew He wanted nothing more.

I struggled to contain my joy. I knew now that I had the chance of a lifetime to tell my story as I told His and that I had the privilege of sharing the gift of love and grace, which Jesus had shared with me. I needed to pass it on. I knew that now I was ready to follow His lead wherever that might take me.

---

35 Compare John 21:15–17.

10

The Story Goes On

Over the next several weeks, Jesus appeared to us on numerous occasions, teaching and comforting us. I cannot remember a greater time of learning and fellowship. I had been given a chance to understand why Jesus was crucified. He said, "None of this caught Me by surprise. I knew what I would have to endure from the beginning of time, yet, because of My love for you, I was willing to pay the price; I was willing to give My life for all who desire to share in the glory of My Father. I knew that many would see and believe, while the hearts of others would be hardened and they would turn away. Yet, I did all of this for those like you who are not satisfied with this life and want something better. I was willing to give My life as payment for yours. The hardest part of my gift was the time of separation from My Father when I did not feel His presence. Though knowing the plan, I had never experienced this before. But now," He said, "the ultimate sacrifice has been made, death has been conquered, and I now stand victorious over the devil as living proof that humans can overcome the darts and

10 The Story Goes On

snares of the enemy when he seeks to discourage and entrap them. Never let anyone steal your joy, for by My blood you have been forgiven and set free. I came to earth for those who are willing to follow Me. Though there were moments when pain and the weight of sin wore heavy on Me, yet My Father sustained Me through My pain. And He will do the same for you in your time of need."[36]

Jesus told us how things will be in the new heaven and the new earth. He shared stories of the riches of time that await us in the Father's kingdom. He explained what we need to do to reach heaven. He asked that we follow in the footprints He has left for us. Yet, if we happen to fall or slip off the pathway, He promised us that the Holy Spirit would restore us to the true way if we will but listen. He also

---

36   See Hebrews 4:16.

told us that the price of our reconciliation has been paid in advance and that we need not worry about tomorrow for He will never leave us or forsake us.

When Jesus finally ascended into heaven, I remembered His earlier words to His disciples: "Let not your heart be troubled; you believe in God, believe also in Me. In My Father's house are many mansions; if it were not so, I would have told you. I go to prepare a place for you. And if I go and prepare a place for you, I will come again, and receive you to Myself; that where I am, there you may be also."[37]

I knew that Jesus' story was not complete. There is another chapter to come. He is now in the sanctuary above, interceding as High Priest for those who have received Him, and someday soon He will come again.[38] Are you ready?

---

37 John 14:1–3, NKJV.
38 See Hebrews 7:25; 9:28.

10 The Story Goes On

Many years after He ascended to heaven, Jesus appeared to the Apostle John on the Isle of Patmos with the promise: "Surely I come quickly."

Our hearts echo John's response — "Even so, come, Lord Jesus."[39]

---

[39] Revelation 22:20.

TEACH Services, Inc.
P U B L I S H I N G

We invite you to view the complete
selection of titles we publish at:
www.TEACHServices.com

We encourage you to write us
with your thoughts about this,
or any other book we publish at:
info@TEACHServices.com

TEACH Services' titles may be purchased in
bulk quantities for educational, fund-raising,
business, or promotional use.
bulksales@TEACHServices.com

Finally, if you are interested in seeing
your own book in print, please contact us at:
publishing@TEACHServices.com

We are happy to review your manuscript at no charge.